MW01231226

Goodnight Wild Heart Ranch

Annette M King

Photos by C. Greg Silva
& Annette King

ISBN-13:
978-1539099147

ISBN-10:
1539099148

This Book Belongs to:

_____

Who promises to be kind to animals

Age_____Date_____

From_____

To all the sleepy children in all the sleepy worlds...

May you have the sweetest dreams of skunks, bunnies and squirrels...

For Katie and David

Every baby and child needs sleep to grow big and strong. You grow the most while you are sleeping. It is time to say goodnight to the animals and for all of you to go to bed.

Goodnight to the opossums who are getting so big!

Goodnight Sherman puppy who sleeps with Abby the pig!

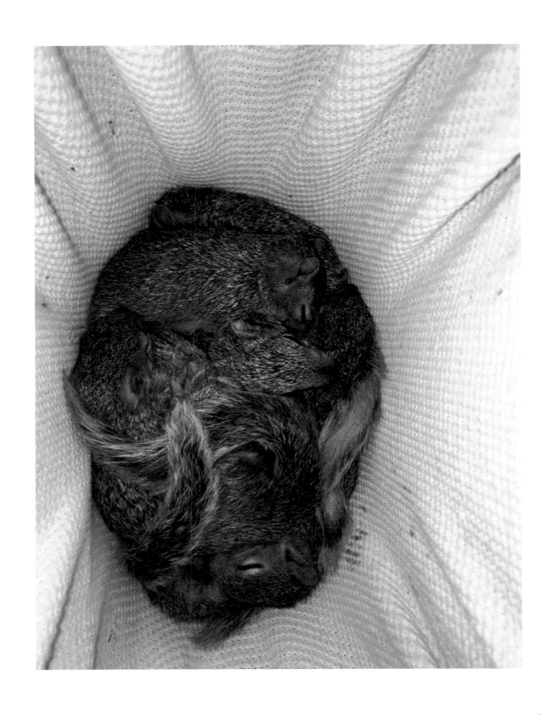

Goodnight little squirrels, I hope you sleep tight.

Goodnight all you opossums, now nobody fight!

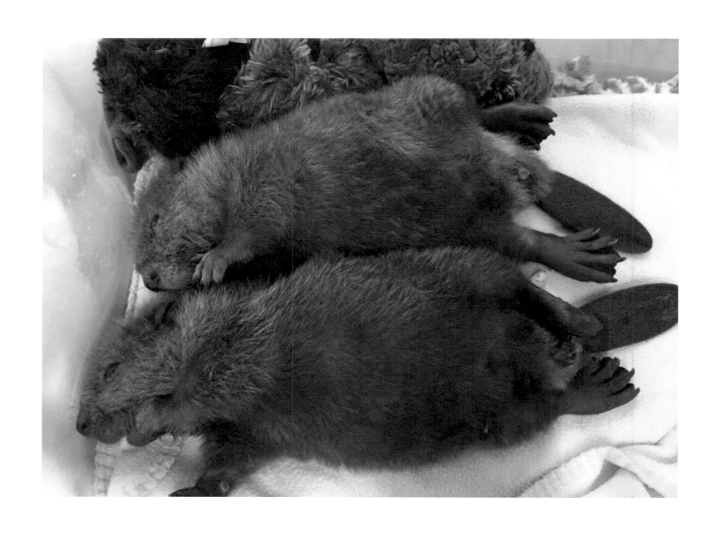

Goodnight beaver babies. Shhhhh!
Don't make a peep.

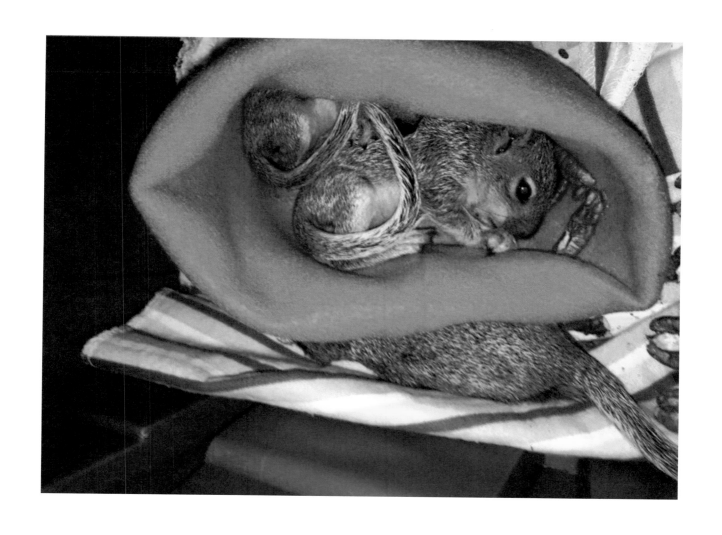

Goodnight to the squirrel who's pretending to sleep.

Goodnight Mr. Falcon. You look wide awake!

Goodnight Mr. Bobcat. Don't stay up too late!

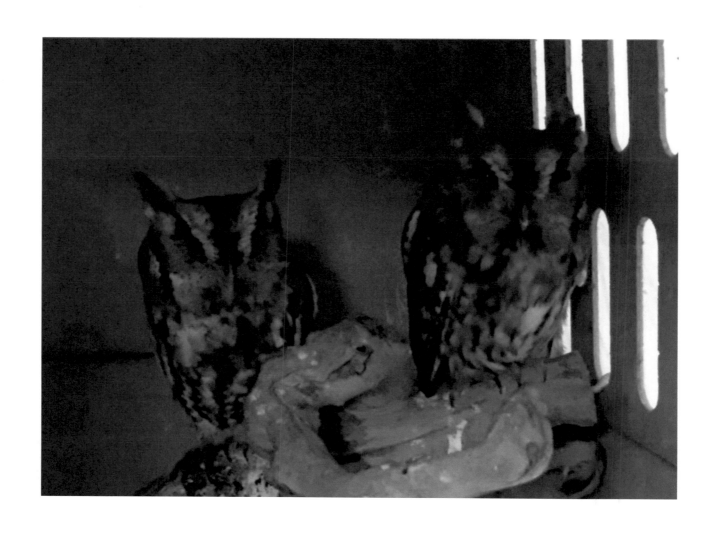

Goodnight little owls who slept all day long.

Goodnight little birds. Time for sleep, not for song.

Goodnight baby cottontails snug in their nest.

Goodnight sleepy raccoon. Now get some good rest!

Goodnight Teddy bird who talks, whistles and toots.

Goodnight Mrs. Owl who gives not a hoot.

Goodnight baby skunks, who don't smell so bad.

Goodnight little owl. WOW! What big eyes that you have!

Goodnight Kiki Monster, now that's a big yawn!

Have the sweetest of dreams and I will see you at dawn.

Hey little squirrels, get back in your bed!

So dreams of trees full of nuts can dance in your head.

Goodnight coyote puppies, so tired from play.

Goodnight little hummingbird. No more humming today!

Goodnight Mr. Turtle, all snug in your shell.

Goodnight little foxes who cuddle so well.

Goodnight Mother Coyote and all of her brood.

Goodnight Keebler the Lemur, who is one awesome dude!

And goodnight to the 'possum who is being so rude!

To all of the fawns, you have a good night.

"Now please stop reading the book and TURN OUT THE LIGHT!"

"FIVE MORE MINUTES MOM PLEASE?"

All the animals in this book were saved by Wild Heart Ranch Wildlife rescue. The wild animals were found as orphans or adults with injuries and were raised and healed by our staff of volunteers and returned to the wild.

Some of the animals like Teddy the parrot, Lumpy the tortoise, Keebler the Lemur and 'Kiki Monster' the Kinkajou are permanent residents who were part of the exotic pet trade and needed a forever home after their owners could no longer care for them. We give these animals a lifetime of love and attention.

Wild Heart Ranch is a nonprofit wildlife rescue located in Rogers County Oklahoma, near Tulsa. We take in all species of wildlife and care for around 3,000 animals each year, and have been in operation since 1996.

wildheartranch.org

About the author;

I founded Wild Heart Ranch many years ago after someone handed over a pair of orphaned raccoons who had nowhere to go for help. Today, I have cared for more than 40,000 wild animals.
This is my final interaction with one of my all-time favorite rescues before his release. Bucky the beaver who grew up without siblings believed I was his mother. He finally found a mate and today lives happily and free in a remote wetlands location.
I always love them enough to let them go and be who they were born to be. They are never 'mine'.
Thanks for helping me say "goodnight"!
-Annette

Made in the USA
Columbia, SC
23 November 2024

46766363R00022